This storybook is dedicated
to
my grandchildren, Asa and Ellis,
and
my husband, Joel,
whose lives inspired me to write this story.

~

Special thank you
to
my family
for encouragement to get this story out,
seeing the value in it, and believing in me.
My daughter, Molly,
who contributed her writing, editing,
and photography skills.

~

My dear friend, Sue Britton,
for her kind words of encouragement,
diving into production needs — making sure
everything was just right,
and for loving Hugo as much as I do!

~

My illustrator, Mary Coon,
who was selected to illustrate but also became my friend.
For giving faces and life to my storybook family
and for bringing my personal life into this story
with such accuracy!

~

I consider this not only my accomplishment—but
all of yours as well.

Thank you.

Published by
Lulu's Little Books

luluslittlebooks.com

Print ISBN: 978-1-09835-158-8

Printed in the United States of America on
SFI Certified paper.

First Edition

HUGO MAKES BREAD
WITH
GRANDAD

JoJo - and Maggie - can you find my puppy Lulu?
Peggy Alberda
May - 2021

The bread I eat at my house looks
different from the bread I eat at
my grandparent's house.

My Grandma and
Grandad *never* buy bread
at the grocery store.
They mix flour and stuff
together and make
their own bread.

Grandad makes oatmeal bread. It's brown and soft and warm.
I call it Grandad Bread.

We put butter on it and watch it melt. Sometimes we squeeze
honey on it but my hair gets sticky when we do.

My grandma makes bread too, but it doesn't look like Grandad's. Her bread is round and white. When she slices it, crumbs get all over the pl

She says she catches yeast that is in the air and keeps it in a sourdough pot. That's what makes her bread poof way up!

Grandad said, "Hey Hugo. I'm about to make some bread,
how about we make it together?"

"Sure Grandad, I will help you!"
We got out the big heavy bowl Grandma keeps
in her laundry room and put it on the counter.
Then Grandad found the stepstool and I climbed up.

In the big bowl we mixed up warm water and honey and yeast.
That's what makes Grandad's bread get poofy.
Grandad says the yeast burps, putting air in the bread
so it grows tall and soft and fluffy.

Then it was time to put in some salt.
I told Grandad that I didn't think
salt would taste good in there.

He told me that it wouldn't taste like bread if we didn't,
so I dumped it in.

Grandad let me stir it up with a big, long, tall spoon
that he made from his apple tree.

He calls it the wooden spoon,
but I call it the apple spoon.
My Grandad makes lots of stuff—he even made
the board that he slices his bread on.
He calls that the breadboard, and I do too.

Grandad poured in the oil. He said I was too little to pour it
but he let me put in lots of oats.
Sometimes he calls it oatmeal. When Mom makes *me*
oatmeal for breakfast, it doesn't look like that. Grandma says
if I want I can just call them oats, so I think I will.

I told Grandad my 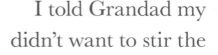 arm was tired and I
didn't want to stir the breadstuff anymore, so
he stirred while I dumped in some flour. Grandad said,

"Add a little more ...more ...more!"
Then poof! There was flour everywhere! All over the floor,
my tummy, my toes and even Grandad's nose!

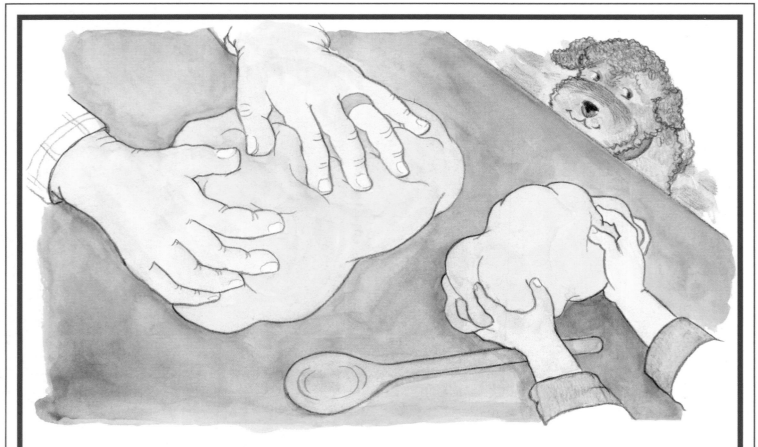

Grandad gave me a little ball of dough and he made
a big ball for himself. He showed me how to push and
fold the dough — He called it kneading.
I like to squish it and watch it squeeze between my fingers.

Grandma went into her laundry room and got a big bread pan for
Grandad's bread and a little one for mine.
My grandma has lots of tiny dishes, cups and teapots just for me.

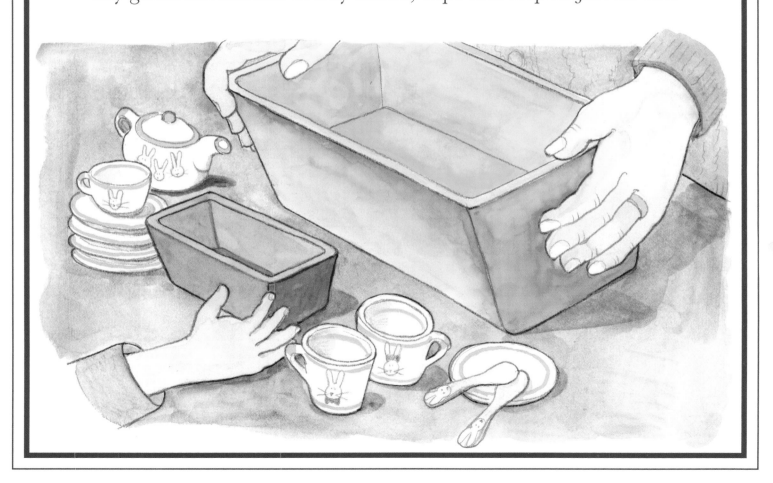

We put oil in our bread pans and our fingers got *really* slippery.
We smeared it all over the pan. Grandad said,
"Oops! Don't put the oil on the outside and don't leave
any dry spots or the bread will stick."

We rolled our dough into a long, fat, hotdog shape and
then plopped it in our pans. Grandma gave us clean
white kitchen towels with a red stripe on the end to cover
our bread. I asked if the bread was going to bed now.
Grandma smiled and said, "I guess it is!"

We put
Grandad's big pan
and my little pan
in the dish cabinet.
Grandma said
the light inside
would make a
nice, warm place
for my bread
to take a nap.

Grandma said it was time for my nap too.

"NOOOOOOOO," I cried,
"Grandad and I are making bread!"

Grandad sat me on his lap and told me this is
the no peeking part. He said if I promised to take
my nap I would see the magic when I got up.
He told me the bread needs quiet time too.

When I woke up,
I ran to the dish cabinet
and peeked in the
little glass windows.
Grandma's cabinet
light glowed on
the white towel
covering our bread.

"Grandad, Grandad," I shouted,
"The magic happened! Hurry! Come see!"
The bread was so much bigger now.
I asked if it was balloon bread and Grandad said
that was a pretty darn good name for it!

Grandma told me it was
time to preheat the oven.
"What does that mean?"
I asked.
She said, "The oven
needs to be nice and
hot before you put
the bread in so it will
bake correctly."
She told me to go play
until it was ready.

I went to the toy box in the
dining room corner where Grandma
keeps my toys and stuff.

I pushed my red
truck around the
table making
the motor noise.
Grandad called
"Come watch
this, Hugo."

I climbed back up
on the step stool.
Grandad took
his knife and put
a cut right in the
top of his bread!

"Don't cut mine!"
I cried."

"I have to," Grandad said, "It makes room for the bread
to expand when it bakes. It might blow a gasket if we don't!"
So I let Grandad cut mine too, but just a little.

Grandad told me to stand back by Grandma.
She put her arm around my shoulder as we watched
Grandad slide the pans into the hot oven.
I could feel the warm air against my cold cheeks.
Grandma let me set the timer.

She said to turn
the timer dial
to the 50, so I did.

"When the bread is done, the timer will ding," she said.
Grandad said, "I don't need a timer!
My nose tells me when it's done!"

Grandad cleaned up the messy kitchen while Grandma read me stories
in her boofie chair. We always read my favorite books when I come visit.
My favorite is about a little bear playing tricks on his grandad
and I like the one about pickles too!

I said, "What's that smell Grandma?" It made my tummy growl.
"That's your bread baking," she said. "It fills the house with the
most wonderful aroma as it changes from dough to bread."

We all peeked in the oven window,
"More magic!" I shouted. "There's real bread in there!"
It was shiny and brown, and it didn't look like dough at all anymore!

Grandad started counting,

5-4-3-2-1

Ding!
...went the timer
just as Grandad
put his finger
in the air!

"Breads done!"
He exclaimed.

I stood back by Grandma again. She tucked me in her arms
and gave me a li'l squeeze.
Grandad put on the funny red mittens so his hands wouldn't
get burned. I guess they are called oven mitts—that's what
Grandma calls them.

Grandad dumped 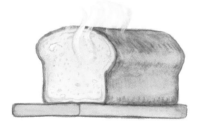 the bread out of the
hot pans then flipped them over with his
red mitts. He told me they would need to
cool down a little before we could eat them.
We read some more stories but I don't remember what
they were called. I just kept thinking about our bread.

Grandma put the dishes and the breadboards on the table
and I got the honey bear. Grandad got out his long shiny knife
that had big teeth on the edge. Grandad says it's *really* sharp
and that I'm not allowed to touch it!

Grandad placed his bread on his big board and put my loaf on a tiny board that he had made just for me. As Grandad sliced the bread, I could see twirly smoke floating up.

Grandma said that was steam — that's how the bread tells us that it is still too hot to eat.

I shared a piece of my little bread with them and Grandad
shared his too. They just put butter on their bread but
I put lots of honey on mine!

My tummy felt warm and happy while we shared our bread at Grandma's table.

I ate the soft part of the bread but left the crust. Grandad said that was his favorite part. He'd bet me a nickel it would be my favorite too someday.

When I get home I'm gonna tell mom making bread
isn't hard like I thought. You just keep putting stuff in a bowl,
then stir it up and smash it around. After it has a nap,
you stay back by Grandma while it goes in the oven.
Then you got bread.

Grandma said I must be growing up, because I didn't lose
interest in the bread making project. Grandad said that I made
him proud. Then he slowly shook his head up and down as
he sat back in his chair and crossed his arms.
He was smiling real big.

At bedtime, Grandma and Grandad knelt next to my bed.
After we thanked God for each other and for our bread,
they kissed me goodnight.
"I will leave the night light on," Grandma whispered
as they tiptoed out of my room.

Tucked in my bed that night, I felt all cozy inside.
I remembered Grandad smiling and
saying that I made him proud.

Hugo's ~~Grandad's~~ Bread

Makes 2 full size loaves in 3 hours

2 packages active dry yeast
½ cup warm water (105 to 115°)
1 ¾ cups warm water
3 Tablespoons honey
1 Tablespoon salt
2 Tablespoons oil
1 cup rolled oats (instant or old fashioned)
5 to 6 cups all-purpose or bread flour
½ to 1 cup additional flour for kneading

Dissolve yeast in ½ cup warm water in a large mixing bowl.
Stir in Additional 1 ¾ cup water, honey, salt, oil, oats and
2 ½ cups of the flour. Mix until smooth.
Slowly incorporate the remaining 2 ½ cups flour.

Knead in a stand mixer for 5 minutes or turn the dough onto
a lightly floured surface and knead by hand 8-10 minutes.
The dough will be sticky, so add additional flour
1 tablespoon at a time, just enough to make it smooth,
elastic and easy to handle.

Knead a few times by hand to form a ball.

Place your dough in a greased bowl then turn the
greased side up. Cover with oiled plastic wrap.
Cover with a clean kitchen towel and let it rise in a
warm place for about one hour. The dough will double in size.

Press down the dough to release the gas inside.
Divide in half. Form dough into two hotdog shape loaves,
place in two bread pans that are coated with spray oil
(no olive oil spray, the bread will stick to the pan).
Cover with the same oiled plastic wrap and towel.

Allow the bread to rise in a warm place until doubled in
size for about one hour.

Position oven rack so bread bakes-in the center of the oven.
Preheat your oven to 425°

When the oven is hot, slowly remove the towel & plastic wrap.
Slash the top 2-3 times with a sharp knife.

Bake for approximately 25 to 30 minutes until the loaves
are deep golden brown. (200° with internal thermometer)
Allow to rest in pans 5 min.
Turn onto a cooling rack.
Let the bread cool for 30-60 minutes before you slice it
to retain moisture.

If you make a small Hugo size loaf, the other two loaves
will be just a bit smaller.

(See web page for more detailed instructions.)
facebook.com/peggyalberdaauthor

Author
Peggy Alberda

Peggy Alberda is a wife, mother, and grandmother. Her friends and family call her an "expert in coziness" with her uncanny ability to make others feel at home. Peggy and her husband Joel make all of their own bread. They have passed this tradition on to their children and now grandchildren. For so many it has been a gift of not only food but of love and home as well. Peggy resides in Indiana with her husband and their Havapoo, Lulu.
facebook.com/peggyalberdaauthor
luluslittlebooks.com

Illustrator
Mary Coons

Mary Coons was born in New Jersey, attended Rutgers College, and has lived all over the United States. She has illustrated 20 books as well as 3 she penned herself. She has drawn nearly five hundred houses, every one full of good memories. Mary is married, has two sons and a dog. She makes her home in Indianapolis.
MaryCoonsDesigns.com

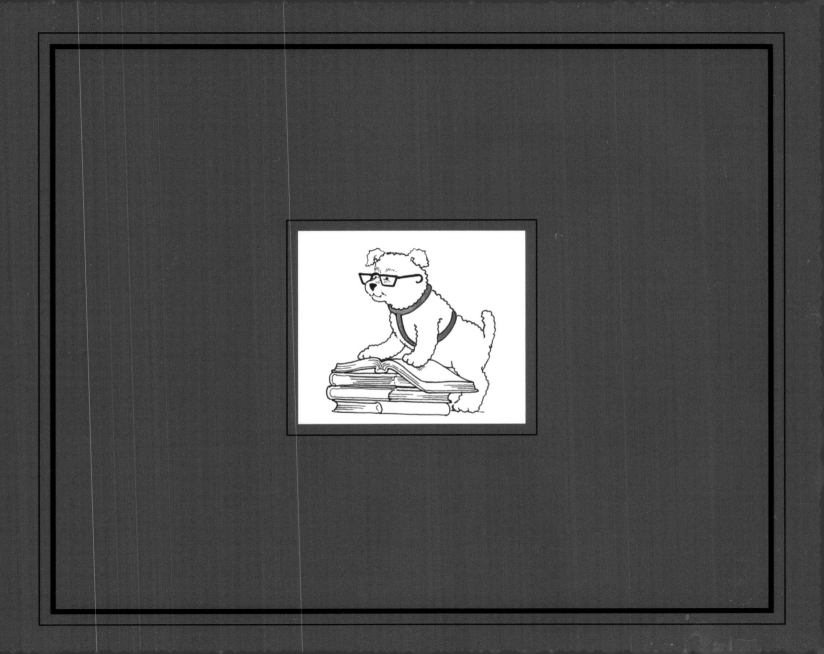